python programming

I0020586

Fluent In python - code Examples, Tips & Trick for Beginners

Contents

Introduction

The following chapters will discuss some of the things that you need to know in order to get started with python programming. The python coding language is one of the best coding languages that you can use as a beginner because it is easy to read, easy to use, and will still give you all the power that you need to write out the codes that you want. This guidebook is going to spend some time helping you learn some of the basics of writing your own codes.

There are a lot of different things that you can add into your python code to make it work the way that you would like. This guidebook will not only talk about some of the basics of getting started with python, but it will also talk about how to work with classes and objects inside the language, how to work with the if statements, how to work with loops, and even how to raise your own exceptions inside of the code. all of these can come together to help you to write a powerful code for games, and other programs that you want to work with.

Working with the python code can be a great experience. It will help you, even as a beginner, learn how to write out your own codes and get the results that you want in no time. When you are ready to write out some computer codes and see results, make sure to read through this guidebook and learn everything that you need to make some of your own   codes.

There are plenty of books on this subject on the market, thanks again for choosing this one! Every effort was made to ensure it is full of as much useful information as possible, please enjoy!

chapter 1: an Introduction to python

Many people are interested in learning a brand-new coding language. They want to be able to work more on the computer, understand how a website works, and even work on creating some of their own programs. But if you have no experience with computer or with coding, where are you supposed to get started? This is one of the hardest parts about starting in coding. There are so many different coding languages you can learn, from Java and JavaScript to c++ and more, which one will be the best to help you get started?

as a beginner, python is considered one of the best options to get you going. This is often considered the beginner's coding language because it is easy to learn and you won't have trouble reading it right from the start. There are many other benefits that come from using this kind of coding language as well, such as the fact that python is considered open sourced so that you won't have to pay anything to use it and anyone can make changes when needed. python can also work on all the operating systems, so you won't have to change the computer that you use just to learn a new coding language.

Despite being a coding language that is simple for beginners to get started with, there is still a lot of power and functionality that comes with working on this language. You will be able to write powerful codes in the process, and when combined with some other coding languages, python can become even stronger. Let's take a look at some more things that you need to know about python and why it may be the best choice for you.

Why Should I Learn python?

Since there are so many different coding languages that you can learn about, you may be curious as to why python would be the best option for you. Many people, beginners and experts alike, will choose to work on python because it is easy to learn, easy to read, and can take on even the most challenging codes that you will want to write. There are many reasons why you would want to work with the python coding language including:

- Readable: python has a language that is really easy to read. In fact, it is considered one of the most readable languages out there, and many beginners are able to read at least some of the code without having to learn anything in the beginning. Since it is so easy to use, many beginners will learn off this one and then can add it in with some other languages if you decide this is needed.
- Free: some computer programs will cost money for you to just use them, but when it comes to using python to code, you will find that it is free. programmers can add this to their computers for free, and they are even allowed to make some modifications to the code and redistribute it without having to pay anything as well. If you get stuck with something, python provides free customer support to help you out.
- Fast: even though python is considered easy enough for an absolute beginner to get started, there is still the benefit of it being a high-level language. This means that when you make programs and codes with this language, you are going to notice that the execution of those codes is nice and fast. There are some coding languages that are a bit slow to execute, but python is fast and will get the work done on time.
- Works on many platforms: you can use python on all of the major operating systems, so you can use whatever computer you want to work with. Linux and Unix are often the systems that most people want to work with, but you can choose to use your Mac oS or Windows computer as well. This makes it easier for you to get to work on the code without having to purchase a new operating system or computer.
- a large library: the library for python is pretty big, so this is going to be very useful for the beginner to work with. You will find that the python library includes codes, functions, and some other options that are needed so that you can get the full functionality of the language. any time that you need a specific thing to happen inside the code, you can just visit this library to help you out.
- a large community: this is really important for someone who is brand new to a coding language. You can go to the community any time that you have some questions, need some ideas, or want to learn something new about the python community. Since there are so many people who will use python, this can be a great place to find the resources that you need.

Many people enjoy working with python because it is so simple and easy to use. Even if you have never worked with a programming language in the past, the python coding language is a good option to start with. Everyone can enjoy it, and you are sure to get all the codes and programs written that you would like.

Download python

Before you are able to work on any of the codings that you would like, you need to make sure that you have the python coding language downloaded on your computer. Since python will work on every operating system, you will just need to turn on your personal computer or the one that you want to use python with, in order to get started.

Since the python coding language is free to use as you would like, you will be able to download it without paying anything. You will just need to go to the python website (www.python.com) and then look to find the version that you need for your personal computer. There are versions for each of the operating systems so read through them and find the one that is right for you. once you click on the option that your computer needs, continue to follow the prompts that come up on your computer to finish the download.

While you do need to download the python program to get the tools that are needed to write out your codes, you need to make sure that a few other things come as well. You need to make sure that the text editor is being downloaded as well (this is the part that you will write out your codes in) and the IDE, which is the environment that is needed to read and execute all of the codes that you write. First is the text editor. You don't need something that is too complicated to get this started. Usually using something like Notepad on Windows or another product that is similar will work just fine.

Don't forget to download the IDE as well. If you don't add the IDE to your computer, you will never be able to write or execute the code at all. There are some options that you can pick with IDE's so you can pick the one that comes with the python download, or you can look around to find another option that has some more features based on what you would like to do with your coding.

once these things are downloaded on your computer, you are ready to get started on writing some of your own codes. The process is simple, but let's take a look at some of the basics that come with the python code to help you to read the syntax a bit better.

Some Basic parts of the python code

as you get to work on your own codes, you will start to notice that there are a lot of different parts that come with them. Understanding some of the basic parts will make it better to understand what is going on in the codes that you are working on. This section is going to spend some time talking about some of the basic parts that come with the python code and why they are so important.

The python keywords

The first part that we will look at is the keywords that come in this language. Like many other coding languages, python is going to have a list of keywords that mean specific actions inside the code, and they should only be used for those purposes, or you will confuse the system. You will find that these keywords are in charge of giving out commands to the compiler so that it reacts the way that you would like. They are reserved to help you execute your code so make sure that you never use them outside of these uses.

Naming your identifiers

When you are working on some codes inside of python, there are going to be things known as identifiers that you often need to use. These have many different names, and we will work on identifying them a bit more as we continue. Some of the names that they are known as include variables, entities, functions, and classes. When you name an identifier, you are able to use pretty much the same rules on all of them, which makes it easier to handle. Some of these rules include:

- Naming these identifiers is simple. You can use both the lower-case and the upper-case letters any time that you would like. Numbers and the underscore symbol are allowed as well. any combination of the above are allowed, just make sure that you aren't adding in spaces in this name. So, you would name it Mypythonprogram rather than My python program.
- The identifiers can't start with any numbers. It is fine to use numbers throughout the name, but you should never have this at the beginning of the name or in the first character at least. This will result in an error when you type it into the compiler so if you are uncertain about why you see an error, check on this part.

- The identifier shouldn't have one of the keywords that we talked about before. Doing this will confuse your compiler so just avoid it.

outside of these simple rules, you can have a lot of freedom in what you would like to name all of your identifiers. If you do happen to forget one of the rules and you name something incorrectly, your compiler will have a syntax error, and you just need to go through and fix it.

Flow of control

another thing that is important for your python code is the flow of control. This helps you to figure out how you will write out that code so that it will work properly. python keeps it simple and will write out the code from top to bottom, just like we are used to reading, so you won't have to worry about it being out of order or anything.

When you are writing out your code, think of it as writing out a grocery list. You will write down the first thing that you want to happen at the top, and then the second and so on until the code is done. It is as simple as that!

Statements

You will use a lot of statements when writing out a code in python. These are useful for your code because they will just be strings of code, which includes some of the other parts we have talked about, that you will send over to the compiler to execute. You can write out pretty much any statement that you would like in your code, as long as it is written out in a way that your compiler is going to understand. You can choose to make a statement short, such as having a few lines with it, or make it longer, there really aren't many   rules   with   it.

comments

at times in your code, you will want to write out something that is known as a comment. These can be helpful to the other programmers who may look through your code and need help understanding what is going on at each point. You will write them out so that those using the code won't have any idea that they are there (they won't affect the functionality of code). Instead, they are like little notes to yourself and to the other programmers to show what is going on.

To write out one of these codes, you will just need to write the (#) sign in front of all your comment. So, you would write out #this is my python code. Then you just skip on to the next line when you want the code to start reading your code again. as long as that sign is in front of the information, the compiler is trained to just skip right over it and won't read anything that you wrote down. You can write out a lot of these codes or just a few depending on how complicated your code is. It is best to not write out too many of these though because it can crowd up the whole code and makes it harder to read.

classes and objects

We will talk about these a bit more in one of the following chapters, but as you work on your python code, you will notice that there are a lot of classes and objects that you will need to work with. The objects are basically the different parts that are found inside of your code while the classes will be the little containers that will hold onto these objects. The classes will help to keep the code more organized.

Now, when you are creating a class, you need to make sure that the objects that you place inside of that class are similar in some way. They can't all be random, but that doesn't mean that you can't have them be a little bit different. When someone looks into your class, they should be able to tell why you placed the objects in there together. For example, you can write out a class for vehicles, and then you would have cars, vans, trucks, and so on. These are not all the same, but most people would have a good idea why they are in the same class.

Functions

Functions are another important part o the python language. This is basically a part of the code that you are able to reuse, and that is often used inside the code just to finish off one action. Functions are great because they are more effective than other options so you can work on your code without wasting time. There are a lot of functions that are found in the python language so you can benefit from this, plus, you are able to write out some of your own functions as well.

When you are working on your code, you will need to make sure that you are defining the function. once you have been able to define the function and it is considered finalized, it is time to execute it to work in the code. You have the choice to call it up from the python prompt, or you can call it up from another function. Below is an example of how you are able to do this:

```
#!/usr/bin/python

# Function definition is here
def print( str ):
   "This prints a passed string into this
function"
   print str

   return;
```

```
# Now you can call printme function
printme("I'm first call to user defined function!")
printme("again second call to the same function")
```

When this is placed into your compiler, you will be able to see the two statements that we wrote out inside of the code come up like a message. This is just one example of how you would call up a function, and you can always change up the statements that are inside the code and figure out how you want them to execute later.

Variables

and now we are going to spend some time talking about variables. Variables are going to be little spots on the memory of your computer that you will reserve to store values of your code. When you create a new variable, you are reserving some space in your memory. In some cases, and with some data types, the interpreter is able to decide where you should store this information to use later on. This helps to speed up the process for you since you will work a lot of data types for your variables including decimals, integers, and characters.

Your job in this process is to make sure that the right values are going to the right variables; this helps you to make sure that it all works inside the code you are working on. You are able to give the variable whatever value you want, but it is best to make sure that these work inside of your code. When you want to assign a value to a variable, you should simply use the equal (=) sign. a good example of how you would do this assignment includes:

```
#!/usr/bin/python

counter = 100        # an integer assignment

miles   = 1000.0     # a floating point

name    = "John"     # a string


print counter
```

```
print miles
print name
```

With this particular example, you are going to get the results that went with the variable that you placed with the value. For example, the counter is going to provide you with 100 for the result, the miles would be 1000, and the name is going to give you the result of John.

as you can see, there are a lot of different parts that can come with your python code. But all of these come together pretty well so that you can make some complex and powerful programs. You will use these quite a bit as you start to work on more of your own codes.

chapter 2: What are classes and objects in the code?

The first topics that we are going to discuss when working on a python code are the objects and classes. These are important because they are going to help you to put everything in the right place with your code. The objects are used to help you define certain parts of the code so that they are organized and pretty easy to understand. For the classes, you use these because they work as containers for the objects. The objects that share something in common are going to end up in the same class because this helps the code   work   more   effectively.

When you are working with your objects, it is important to understand that whenever they are placed together into the same class, you can do this with anything that you would like. of course, for this to work the best, they need to have some similarity to each other before they are placed into that class. This helps the code to stay in order a bit more. Think about it like organizing the kitchen or your closet. You want to make sure that all of the shoes are in one area, the clothes are hung up together, the purses placed in the corner together, and other items grouped so that it is easier for you to find them later on. The classes that are created can have any object that you would like, but it is best if they are grouped because they are similar in some way so that the program works better.

To keep things simple, the objects are going to be different parts of the code that you are writing, and then the classes will be like the boxes or the containers that can hold onto these objects, objects that have something similar to each other, so they aren't just rolling around together. You will need to label these classes as well to help them work better, but pick out a name that makes sense for the information inside. Remember that while the objects need to be similar, they don't need to be identical when they are inside of the same class. people who look at these objects should understand why they go together, but they don't have to be exactly the same.

If you are working on learning a new programming language, objects and classes are a good way to help you learn more while also making sure that you keep your information organized inside of the code. It is your job to learn how to create these classes properly, and you place the objects inside of it, you will see that your codes will work out better.

creating a New class

Now that we know a bit more about the objects and the classes, it is time to learn how to create one of these new classes because you will need to do that quite a bit of this with your codes. When you want to create a statement for one of these classes, you need to take some time to create a brand-new definition as well. You need to place the keyword in first and then add in the name of the class right after this. This is followed with the superclass being inside some parenthesis. another thing to look at is that the end of this first line needs to be a semicolon. This isn't really required because your code will still work with it, but you will find that it is considered proper coding etiquette to add this in.

all of this may be a little bit confusing, so let's take a look at the example below to see how we would create a new class inside of python:

```
class Vehicle(object):
#constructor
def_init_(self, steering, wheels, clutch, breaks, gears):
self._steering = steering
self._wheels = wheels
self._clutch = clutch
self._breaks =breaks
self._gears  = gears

#destructor
def_del_(self):
    print("This is destructor....")


#member functions or methods
def Display_Vehicle(self):
```

```
        print('Steering:' , self._steering)

        print('Wheels:', self._wheels)

        print('clutch:', self._clutch)

        print('Breaks:', self._breaks)

        print('Gears:', self._gears)

#instantiate a vehicle option
myGenericVehicle = Vehicle('power Steering', 4, 'Super clutch', 'Disk Breaks', 5)

myGenericVehicle.Display_Vehicle()
```

You should take a moment to open up your compiler and write out this code. as you work on it, you should notice that there are some different parts that show up inside o the code. The first one is going to be the definition of the object, the definition of the method, the destructor function, and the different attributes that are in the code. You will also notice that there are some regular functions and the class function that show up as well. Since some of these are pretty important to the code, we are going to take a moment to talk about them.

class Definition

First on the list is class definition. You will need to write out the object instantiation and the class definition to write out the syntax of your code. These will be important because they tell your compiler what you want to do and the commands that it will need to follow. If you would like to invoke the new class definition with your code, it is simple to just add in the object.attribute or the object.method() function to make this happen.

Special attributes of the code

In addition to working on the class definition, there are also some special attributes that you will have recognized inside your python code. You should take some time to learn what these are because they really do make a difference in the code that you are working on. You will find that these give you some peace of mind of already knowing when the attributes will be seen and that they will be used in the proper way inside the code. There are quite a few attributes that are considered special inside the python code, but the ones that we are going to pay attention to include the following:

__bases__: this is considered a tuple that contains any of the superclasses

__module__: this is where you are going to find the name of the module, and it will also hold your classes.

__name__: this will hold on to the class name.

__doc__: this is where you are going to find the reference string inside the document for your class.

__dict__: this is going to be the variable for the dict. Inside the class name.

accessing members of the class

To get the compiler to recognize the class and execute the parts of the code that you would like, you need to make sure that the code is set up to access all of the members of your classes. There are a few options that you can use to make this happen. all of the methods will work well, the accessor method is the one that is the most often used because it will provide the information inside of the syntax and makes things easier. Let's take a look at a code that will show us how to get this done:

```
class cat(object)
        itsage = None
        itsWeight = None
        itsName = None
        #set accessor function use to assign values to the fields or member vars
        def setItsage(self, itsage):
        self.itsage = itsage
```

```python
def setItsWeight(self, itsWeight):
    self.itsWeight = itsWeight

def setItsName(self, itsName):
    self.itsName =itsName

#get accessor function use to return the values from a field
def getItsage(self):
    return self.itsage
def getItsWeight(self):
    return self.itsWeight

def getItsName(self):
    return self.itsName
```

```python
objFrisky = cat()
objFrisky.setItsage(5)
objFrisky.setItsWeight(10)
objFrisky.setItsName("Frisky")
print("cats Name is:", objFrisky.getItsname())
print("Its age is:", objFrisky.getItsage())
print("Its weight is:", objFrisky.getItsName())
```

If you take some time to place this into your compiler, you will get some results right away. It will state that the name of the cat is Frisky (unless you put in another name there), that the age is 5 and the weight is 10. This is based on the information that we just used inside our code. You can easily change up any of the information or even add to it if you would like by using the basic syntax that is provided above.

Using classes is one of the best ways for you to take all of the information in the code and put it together, so it makes sense. You will need to go through and place your objects inside of the classes for this to work, and the objects do need to be similar in some way, but this is an easy way for you to keep things organized when you are working in python.

chapter 3: The "If Statements" in python

The decision control statements, which are also known as the if statements are the next topic that we will talk about when writing your own python code. In some cases, you want your python code to make some decisions for you based on the information that the user provides to you. For example, if you are working on a game and the user is allowed to put in a few options, you can choose how the program is going to react based on the answer that the user will put into it.

There are a few different types of these if statements. With the most basic one, you will only have the computer respond if the user puts in the right answer. So if you want them to put in an age that is 18 or above, and they place that age in, they will get a message or allowed into the system. But if they put in an age that is considered wrong, the most basic of the if statements will just kick them out of the program. of course, this is not always the best option for your program, and you can expand out the if statements so that you can have a response no matter what answer the user gives to you.

To get started, we will keep it pretty simple for this topic and start out with the most basic of the if statement. This is going to be the easiest and the simplest form of these decision control statements because, with this one, the program will only proceed if the user puts in the answer that you list as correct. In this case, I the user puts in the wrong answer, which will be determined by the conditions that you set ahead of time, the program is going to stay blank. as you can imagine right now, there are some limitations to using this method, but it will help you to get the basics of how these statements work. a simple example of the if-statement includes:

```
age = int(input("Enter your age:"))
if (age <=18):
        print("You are not eligible for voting, try next election!")
print("program ends")
```

Let's take a look at the code above. There are going to be a few things that you will see happen. If your user is in the program and they say that they are 18 years or under, the program will continue to work, and they will see the message "You are not eligible for voting, try next election!". When the user sees this on the screen, the program right now is set to just stop working, but we can add in something else as well if we want. on the other hand, if your user puts in an age that is above 18, they are not going to get a result. Their age is not necessarily wrong here, but since it doesn't meet the criteria that you set.

So, with this program, if the user goes through and puts in that their age is 25, the program can tell that this doesn't meet the conditions that you set. Because the conditions are not met at this point, your program is set up to just end right here. Later we will move on to being able to accept both types of answers and the results that you would like to have shown up for each one, but right now, the program sees that the condition doesn't   match   up   and   then   closes   things   down.

Now, there are going to be a lot of times when you would want the code to respond to any answer that the user gives to it. The user is allowed to put in that their age is 25 or some other number, and having the program just end doesn't make much sense here. This is when we are going to move on to what is known as the if…else statement. With this one, if the conditions are not met, the program will move on to the second part and will execute what you place in there. Let's take a look at how the if…else statements work inside of python:

```
age = int(input("Enter your age:"))
if (age <=18):
        print("You are not eligible for voting, try next election!")
else

        print("congratulations! You are eligible to vote. check out your local polling
station to find out more information!)
print("program ends")
```

This option is going to open up a lot more doors than what you were able to do with just the if statement on its own. There are going to be two options that come up with this one (although you will later learn how to accept more than one answer as well). If the user goes through and types in that they are 17 or a younger age, the statement about them being too young to vote will come up. But this statement goes a bit further and has an option for those who list that they are older than 18. When the user places in a number like this, the second statement in our code is going to show up.

You do have a lot of freedom when you are working on the if…else statements. You can add in a few of these options, and you will be able to change up the statements that show up to fit into the code that you are creating. This basically makes it so much easier for you to react to your users no matter what they put in as an answer.

Now, the example above of the if…else statements is pretty simple, and it is possible for you to go through and add in more steps to the code as well. For example, if you want to allow the user to put in more than two answers, such as three or four options, you can do this will just some more parts to the code. You could choose to have a different message come up for those who are in the 16 to 18 age group, one that is for those who are 19 to 25 years old, and another for those who are at least 26 years old. There are a lot of possibilities that you can use, you just need to look at the program that you want to work with and then split it all up based on what will work the best for your code.

The elif statements

The next if statement we are going to take a look at is known as the elif statements. We spent some time looking at how the basics of the if statements and the if…else statements, both of which can add some interaction in the code between you and the user. But there are some other things that you may want to have to happen with your code, such as letting the user pick from a list of options that will come up for them. If you want to make this list of options come up, the elif statement can be the right one for you.

Elif statements are so easy to use, and you can easily add in more of these statements to your code if you would like. The example that we are going to use will have three options and then a catch all if the user doesn't like any of the answers, but you could add in 20 of these if you would like. In some cases, your elif statement is just going to have a few options for the user to pick from, but in some codes, you need to provide many more options to have this work. The nice thing about the elif statements is that you are able to add in as many as the code needs as long as you write it all out in the proper way.

Let's take a look at how the elif statement is going to work. Remember that this option is pretty simple and you can make them as complicated as your program needs:

```
print("Let's enjoy a pizza! ok, let's go inside pizzahut!")
print("Waiter, please select pizza of your choice from the menu")
pizzachoice = int(input("please enter your choice of pizza:"))
if pizzachoice == 1:
        print('I want to enjoy a pizza napoletana')
elif pizzachoice == 2:
        print('I want to enjoy a pizza rustica')
elif pizzachoice == 3:
        print('I want to enjoy a pizza capricciosa')
else:
        print("Sorry, I do not want any of the listed pizza's, please bring a coca cola for me.")
```

When this code comes up on the screen, your user will be able to take a look and make up their mind on the choices they want. The user can simply pick out the corresponding number to go with this. For example, if they would like to order a pizza napoletana, they would simply need to press number one to make this happen. Then there was also an option at the end of this elif statement code so if the user doesn't want to use any of those pizzas as their choice, they can still get a drink to enjoy. This option just has three options and then the catch all if they don't want any of the pizza options, but the programmer can add in more pizza options if they would like.

and that is really all there is to the decision control statements or the if statements. These can really add some more power to the code and allows for some interaction between the program and the user without you needing to be there at the time. The user can pick out what answer suits their needs the best, and the program will be set up to react in a certain way. You can keep it simple with the if statement and only allow the user to pick one right answer, use the if…else statement so that they can have a few different results based on what they want to put in or the elif statements that will provide the user with the options that are acceptable. There is just so much that these statements can open up and learn how to use the if statements will help you to see results in your own program.

chapter 4: Working with Inheritance codes

The next topic that we are going to talk about is known as inheritance codes. These will save you some time whenever you want to reuse parts of the code without having to write things out quite as much. May of the object oriented programming, or oop, languages, will use this because you can reuse the code while also making some adjustments to some of the code as well. It basically saves you time, is more efficient, and will make the code easier to read. as a beginner, this is a great thing to learn how to use because you won't have to write out as much over time.

To keep things simple, an inheritance is going to be when you take some part of the code you are working on and then turn it into a second class. Inside this second class, you are going to have the exact information as you did from the first class, but you can change some things up and make it work how you want, without ever having to worry about the first class clanging. You can choose to do this with just one time, or you can make a big string of code depending on what you are working with. The inheritance makes this quick and easy to do, and you will enjoy how nice the whole code will look.

To get started with the idea of inheritances, we need to stop and take a look at the base class, which is also known as the first class, and we will use him to create the derived class, which is known as the second class, with the help of these inheritances. It is going to look like the following:

```
#Example of inheritance
#base class
class Student(object):
        def__init__(self, name, rollno):
        self.name = name
        self.rollno = rollno
#Graduate class inherits or derived from Student class
class GraduateStudent(Student):
```

```python
        def __init__(self, name, rollno, graduate):
        Student__init__(self, name, rollno)
        self.graduate = graduate

def DisplayGraduateStudent(self):
        print"Student Name:", self.name)
        print("Student Rollno:", self.rollno)
        print("Study Group:", self.graduate)

#post Graduate class inherits from Student class
class postGraduate(Student):
        def __init__(self, name, rollno, postgrad):
        Student__init__(self, name, rollno)
        self.postgrad = postgrad

        def DisplaypostGraduateStudent(self):
        print("Student Name:", self.name)
        print("Student Rollno:", self.rollno)
        print("Study Group:", self.postgrad)

#instantiate from Graduate and postGraduate classes
        objGradStudent = GraduateStudent("Mainu", 1, "MS-Mathematics")
        objpostGradStudent = postGraduate("Shainu", 2, "MS-cS")
        objpostGradStudent.DisplaypostGraduateStudent()
```

When you type this into your interpreter, you are going to get the results:

('Student Name:', 'Mainu')
('Student Rollno:', 1)
('Student Group:', 'MSc-Mathematics')
('Student Name:', 'Shainu')
('Student Rollno:', 2)
('Student Group:', 'MSc-cS')

overriding The Base class

The next thing that we are going to look at is how to override a base class. There are going to be a few occasions when you are writing a new derived class when you will need to go in and override what is in this base class. What this basically means is that you are going to take a look at what is inside of the base class and then replace some of the behavior, which makes it possible for this new behavior to be available inside the new child case that we are creating.

This can sound a little bit complicated, but it is nice because you will be able to pick and choose the parental features that you need in the derived class, which ones you want to keep, and which ones you want to get rid of when you make a new class. This whole process will help you to make some changes to your new class while you still keep around whatever original parts from the base class that you want. and with the help of using the override method, you won't have to deal with duplicating code and getting the code stuck along the way. It is a simple way to keep the parts that you want, get rid of the parts that aren't working, and make your code behave the way that you want.

overloading

You may also want to consider working with the process known as overloading when working with the inheritances. When you are working on the process of overloading, you will take one of your identifiers and then use it to define two or more methods. For the most part, these will be just two methods that are in the class, but there are times when it can be linked with more than the two. The two methods will have to be inside the same class, but you need to give them each different parameters to keep them separate. You will find that you will want to use this method when you want the two matched methods to go through the same tasks, but you want to make sure that they follow different types of parameters.

Since you are a beginner, it is not common that you will go through the process of overloading because it isn't all that common to start with. But it is still a good idea to learn a bit about it in case you see it in some codes that you borrow for your program. If you do need to go through and work on overloading, it is a good idea to go through and download the extra module that comes with python that is responsible for getting the overloading done.

More Than one Inheritance

It is also possible for you to work on more than one inheritance. This means that you are able to make a line of inheritances that all share some similarities and which will be able to have changes made to them as well. You will notice that the multiple inheritances are going to be similar to a normal inheritance, but you will pretty much take it another step further. When using multiple inheritances, you are going to take one class and then give it at least two or more parent classes to help design it. This is important for growing the code, but you can do this without having to worry about having a mess when you write out the code.

Working on multiple inheritances may sound complicated, but it is a pretty simple process. When you are working with these types of inheritances, you will create a new class, which we will call class3, and this class was created from the features that were inside of class2. Then you can go back a bit further and will find that class2 was created with the features that come from class1. Each layer is going to contain features from the class that was ahead of it, and you can really go down as far as you would like. You can have ten of these classes if you would like, with features from the past parent class in each one, if you would like, as long as it works inside your code.

one thing to remember when you are working on your code and adding in some multiple inheritances is that python is not going to allow for a circular inheritance. You are allowed to use as many of these parent classes as you would like, but you won't be able to go through and make the classes go around in a circle or python will get mad at what you are trying to do. Expanding out the example above to make a class4 and then a class5 and so on are all allowed and can work well, but you need to make sure that you go through and copy out all of the codes in the proper way before making any changes for this to work.

You will find that working with inheritances, especially multiple inheritances is going to be a popular thing to work with inside of python coding. There are quite a few times when you will be able to stick with the same block of code in the program and then make whatever changes you want without having to rewrite everything and make it look like a mess. With the help of inheritances, you are able to write the code out as many times as you want and make changes more efficiently than you did before.

chapter 5: How to Handle Exceptions in Your code

as you are working on your code in python, there will be some occasions when you can add in some exceptions to the code. This is something that you may not have heard about before, and it is a bit confusing in the process, but it is important to understand and learn how to work with exceptions so that your codes work the way that you would like. There are going to be some exceptions that are already found in the python code, and if you raise them, the system will let you know. and depending on the type of code that you are writing, you may want to go through and add in some of your own exceptions as well so that users aren't able to do certain things. Let's take a little look at how exception handling will work so you can use it in your own computer programming.

If there is ever an abnormal condition that will go on with your code, either one that the python compiler already recognized or that you are setting up to work personally on the program that you are creating, you need to use the idea of exceptions inside your code. as we have briefly mentioned, there are going to be a few exception conditions that the compiler will already recognize, and if they are used, the code won't allow the program to finish. For example, if you are adding in the wrong kind of statement to the code, or you misspell one of your classes so the compiler can't find it, or you try to divide by zero, the compiler won't be able to deal with this request and the exception is going to be raised.

These are just a few examples of the types of exceptions that the compiler is going to raise for you. In addition, you are going to run into times when you would like to change around the program that you are working on and you want it to raise an exception. These kinds of exceptions are technically just fine with the interpreter, but according to what you want the program to finish with, you will want the code to raise these exceptions.

an example of this is when you are working on a more adult themed website. You only want to allow users who are at least 21 years old to be able to get on the website. as the programmer, you could raise up an exception that will show up if your user happens to put their age in as 20 or younger. When this happens, you will raise the exception and your code will know not to let the person get through to the website.

as you work through your programming with python, it is a good idea to look through the library that is provided. You should notice that inside of this library, there are a few exceptions that are already accepted there. These are good to know because they will make code writing more efficient and you can use them anytime that you need for your own code writing. one of the most common exceptions that show up in the python language is when you try to divide by zero. You may also run into the issue of trying to read a point that is past where the current file is located. Either of these will cause an exception to be raised in the code.

In addition to what we have talked about so far, there will be times when you want to allow some things to happen and this is where exception handling is going to be the most useful. For example, if you just leave the code alone, if someone goes through and tries to divide by zero, the exception handling will just put up an error message and then the program will close down. If you are in a code, you don't want to have something new show up rather than having a blank computer screen. With the idea of exception handling, you can have a new message come up so that the user knows what is going on and why the computer has an error. For example, you could write out a message that says "You are trying to divide by zero!" rather than just closing out the system.

While the dividing by zero exception is one of the most popular exceptions that you will see, you can also add in some of your own exceptions, even if you don't already see these present inside the python library. While the code is going to add in the exception at times, there will be times when you will go through and add in some of these errors on your own while also determining how you would like your compiler to react when the user brings up these exceptions.

It is important to have a good idea of some of the exceptions that are already found in the python library, so you know which ones you are able to use. Some of these exceptions include:

- Finally — this is the action that you will want to use to perform cleanup actions, whether the exceptions occur or not.
- assert — this condition is going to trigger the exception inside of the code
- Raise — the raise command is going to trigger an exception manually inside of the code.
- Try/except — this is when you want to try out a block of code and then it is recovered thanks to the exceptions that either you or the python code raised.

Raising an Exception

Now that you know what an exception is all about and when you would like to use them inside of the code you that you are writing, it is time for us to learn how we can raise the exceptions inside of the code. If you are going through the code and notice that there is an issue with it or that your program is doing something that seems a bit wrong, you will see that the compiler is going to say something about this and the exception will be raised. This is because the program while reading through the code, is having trouble figuring out what it wants you to do in this situation. Sometimes the issue is pretty simple, such as seeing that you mistyped the name for one of your files, or it could be something like trying to divide by zero.

Let's look at an example where your compiler is going to raise an exception against what you are trying to do inside of the code. This would look like the following:

```
x = 10
y = 10
result = x/y #trying to divide by zero
print(result)
```

The output that you are going to get when you try to get the interpreter to go through this code would be:

```
>>>
Traceback (most recent call last):
        File "D: \python34\tt.py", line 3, in <module>
        result = x/y
ZeroDivisionError: division by zero
>>>
```

For this particular example, the program is raising up an error for you because, in the code, you tried to write out that you wanted the code to divide by zero. as we have talked about a few times, dividing by zero is something that the python code is not going to allow, so you end up getting an error. Now, if you do try to get through and run the program, you are not going to want this error message to show up because it can look a bit messy and unprofessional inside of your code, so you want to make some changes.

The good news is that you do have a few options that you can work with that add something to the code while also letting you choose what is going to happen when these exceptions are shown, rather than the messy error message. You could change up the message that comes up in the error box, for example, or you can even tell the code to react differently rather than showing up the error message in the first place.

often as a beginner, you will want to choose to have a message come up on your screen so that the user knows what is going on and why the exception is being raised. When you write out your own messages, it helps the code to seem friendlier than a confusing exception message, and it makes it easier for the user to make changes that will move the code along. To see what happens when you change the message that comes up when an exception occurs includes:

```
x = 10
y = 0
result = 0
try:
        result = x/y
        print(result)
```

except ZeroDivisionError:
    print("You are trying to divide by zero.")

Now you should notice that this code is going to be pretty similar to what you had above, but it is really easy to change up the message that comes up. With this one, you are going to have an error come up, just like you did before, but you are able to get an easy message to come up, one that the user will be able to understand, rather than the messy message that we had in the last example. You are able to write in any message that you would like in here, but the whole point is to keep it nice and simple, let the user know what went wrong, and then helps the user to make the changes that are needed to move on with the code.

Defining Your own Exceptions

The next thing that we are going to look at is how you can raise some of your own exceptions. In the examples that we did before, we spent some time discussing what will happen when the compiler sees an issue in the code, and it doesn't know how to handle it. But sometimes you are going to work on your own code, and you will want to add in some special exceptions to help it work the way that you want. These exceptions are often going to be just fine with the compiler, and the compiler won't see anything wrong with what you are writing out, but you need to raise the errors based on how the program should work.

For example, you may be working on a code, and you want to make sure that the user is not allowed to put in some numbers while others are going to be just fine. In this example, it would be your job to add in an exception for this. You could be working on a game in your programming, and you want to make sure that the user is only able to make a guess for three times, so you will raise a new exception to handle all of this. The compiler would be fine with the user making as many guesses as they want in this example, but you are able to raise an exception to control how the program works.

as the programmer, you are the one who can create whatever rules that you want to dictate how the code is going to work. any time that you want to make a condition abnormal in your program, you just need to make sure that you go through the process of raising an exception. Let's take a look at how to create these exceptions so that you can use them any time that you need inside your own codes:

```
class customException(Exception):
def_init_(self, value):
        self.parameter = value
def_str_(self):
        return repr(self.parameter)

try:
        raise customException("This is a customError!")
except customException as ex:
        print("caught:", ex.parameter)
```

In this code, you have been successful in setting up your own exceptions and whenever the user raises one of these exceptions, the message of "caught: This is a customError!" is going to come up on the screen. This is the best way to show your users that you have added in a customer exception into the program, especially if this is just one that you personally created for this part of the code, and not one that the compiler is going to recognize on its own.

Now, for the example that we used above, we stuck with some generic wording for the exception to keep it pretty easy. The good news is that you are able to make changes as you need and add in whatever message you need to make the exception work. You can choose to write out something else if you would like, such as "You have to be 18 to use this program" or another message based on what your exception is all about.

Exception handling is so important once you get started on working on some of your own codes. There are many times when you will want to add in an exception to the code that you are writing and learning how to do this and write out the right messages will help it to go so much better. If you feel that the code you are going to write will need some of these exceptions, then you should take some time to type these examples into your compiler to get a little bit of experience in the process!

chapter 6: How Loops can Save You Time

Earlier we spent some time talking about the decision control statements and how these statements will work to help you interact with the user a bit more. But there are still some limitations that are found in the if statements. This is where the loops are going to come into play. These loops are going to be helpful when you are working on a program that needs to repeat itself inside the code, but you don't really want to write out the code all those times. For example, you could work it out so that your code will list out all of the numbers from 1 to 10. You don't really want to go out and write the same code ten times so that all of these numbers show up. Using the idea of a loop would help python to get this done with just a small block of code, saving you time and making the code much easier   to   read.

While there is a lot of information found inside of these loops, they are pretty simple to work with. These loops will just tell the compiler to keep going back through the same part of the code over again until a condition (which you will set up in the code) has been met. If you are trying to get the code to count from one to ten, you simply need to tell the code that it can stop counting once it gets to ten. This is pretty easy to accomplish, and we can look at a few examples to help you get started.

one thing that you have to remember when working on these codes is that you do need to set your condition before running the program. If you forget to set these conditions, you are going to get the program stuck in a continuous loop that is stuck. Double check any of the codes that you write that have loops inside of them so that you make sure the program   moves   on   once   the   loop   is   all   done.

as you work through your python code, you may find that there are a few different types of loops that you are able to work with. We will spend some time talking about the most common loop types that will work for most of the codes that you want to write.

The While Loop

The first loop that we are going to look at is called the while loop inside the python code. This loop is a good one to use if you know ahead of time how often the code should go through the cycles. If you just want the code to go for a few rounds before moving on, you would want to use the whole code. any time that you don't want the loop to have the potential of going through the cycles an indefinite amount of times, you can write down some conditions that will tell the loop when to stop, and the while loop can help with this. and if you want to make sure that the loop is going to go through the process at least one time to check if the results are true or false, you will want to use the while loop. Let's take a look at an example of how this can work to help it make a little more sense:

#calculation of simple interest. ask user to input principal, rate of interest, number of years.

```
counter = 1
while(counter <= 3):
        principal = int(input("Enter the principal amount:"))
        numberofyeras = int(input("Enter the number of years:"))
        rateofinterest = float(input("Enter the rate of interest:"))
        simpleinterest = principal * numberofyears * rateofinterest/100
        print("Simple interest = %.2f" %simpleinterest)
        #increase the counter by 1
        counter = counter + 1
        print("You have calculated simple interest for 3 time!")
```

Take a little bit of time to place this into your compiler and let the code execute. When this is done, you should notice that the output is going to come out so that the user is able to place their information, any information that they want, inside so that it is computed. This one is about interest rates, so the user is able to figure out their interest rates and the final amount based on how much they are purchasing and how much the interest rate is. We have set it up so that the loop is going to go through the motions three times, but if you would like to allow the user to go more than that, you can as well.

The For Loop

The next type of loop that we are going to use is known as the for loop. This one is a bit different than the while loop, but it can be extremely useful in a lot of the codes that you want to write. In fact, the for loop is considered the traditional way for you to write out your loops, so it is a good one to learn how to use.

When you are using the for loop, the user isn't able to go into the code and give it the information, and they won't be able to determine when these loops will start. But with the for loop, python is going to go through the iteration in the order that it shows up inside of your statement, and then this is going to show up on the screen in front of you. It does not need any input from someone else, and it will just keep on going until it reaches the end. an example of how you would use the for loop includes the following:

```
# Measure some strings:
words = ['apple', 'mango', 'banana', 'orange']
for w in words:
print(w, len(w))
```

Now, when you are working on the above example, you can place the information inside of your code, and then when it executes, the program is going to list out the four fruits that are on the screen, keeping them in the same order that you wrote them out. If you want them to show up in a different order than what they show above, you need to write them out differently; the code is not going to do that for you. once the words are placed in the syntax, and you execute the code, you will not be able to make these changes so be careful with this one.

The Nested Loop

The final loop type that we are going to take a look at because it can be helpful with a lot of different codes in python is known as the nested loop. When you are working with a nested loop, you will take one of the basic loops from before and place it inside of another loop. Both of these loops will be given permission to run until they are complete. There are a few times when doing this can be useful in your code, such as when you would like to write out a new multiplication table that will start with one and goes up to ten. Let's take a look at how you would write out this kind of nested loop in your code:

#write a multiplication table from 1 to 10
For x in xrange(1, 11):
        For y in xrange(1, 11):
        print '%d = %d' % (x, y, x*x)

When you got the output of this program, it is going to look similar to this:

1*1 = 1

1*2 = 2

1*3 = 3

1*4 = 4

all the way up to 1*10 = 2

Then it would move on to do the table by twos such as this:

2*1 =2

2*2 = 4

and so on until you end up with 10*10 = 100 as your final spot in the sequence

These are some of the most basic loops that you would want to use when you are working on your own code inside of the python language, and they can be used for many different reasons. You can use it to clean up the code a bit even if you want the same bit of code to keep on running over and over again. It is also a lot simpler to work on than the if statements when you want the same action to keep on happening. Your code will look a lot better, but there will still be a lot of power behind it if you use one of the loop options   above.

chapter 7: add Something New to the code with operators

The last topic that we are going to discuss is that of the operators. These operators can make the code a bit stronger, and there are quite a few different operators that you are able to use. You can use these operators to do a variety of things including giving a value to your variable, comparing parts of your code together, and even mathematical equations. It is all going to depend on what you would like your code to be able to do. Let's take some time to look at these different operators and how they can work inside of your code.

arithmetic operators:

The first type of operators that are often used is known as the arithmetic operators. These are pretty basic to use and will be used any time that wants to work with a mathematical equation. For example, you could use it in order to add together two operands inside of your code There are some basic options that you are able to use with the arithmetic operators including:

- (+): this is the addition operator and it is responsible for adding together both of your values.

- (-): this is the subtraction operator and it is going to be responsible for taking the right operand and subtracting it from the left.

- (*): this is the multiplication operator, and it is used to multiply two or more values in the equation.
- (/): this is the division operator and it is going to divide the value of the left operand from that on the right and gives you the answer.

You get some choices when you are working with this as well. You can choose to write out a statement that just has one of these operators inside of them, or you could add in a few of them. For example, it is fine to add three numbers together inside of your code, or you can multiply a few and subtract some others. If you are using more than one of the arithmetic operators in your code, remember that you will need to use the method of operations. This means that you start with the multiplication, go on to the division and then end with the addition and the subtraction. This is how the compiler will do the work to ensure that you are getting the right answers.

comparison operators

another type of operator that is commonly used inside of python is known as the comparison operator This one is going to be helpful when you want to compare together two or even more values and statements inside the code you are writing. You will often see these used with the Boolean expressions because they operate on the idea of true or false results; you are either going to have the numbers or the statements equal each other, or they won't, and that is all you need to do with them. The comparison operators that you will use inside of python include:

- (>=): this one means to check if the left-hand operand is greater than or equal to the value of the one on the right.

- (<=): this one means to check if the value of the left-hand operand is less than or equal to the one on the right.

- (>): this one means to check whether the values of the left side are greater than the value on the right side of the code.
- (<): this one means to check whether the values of the left side are less than the values that are on the right side.
- (!=): this is the not equal to operator.
- (==): this one is the equal to operator.

as you get to work on your code, you will notice that there are quite a few times when you will want to add in a comparison operator. You often will set up some conditions that need to be met in order for the code to act in a certain way. Then when the user puts in their information, you can use the comparison operators to tell if the user input is the same or different from the conditions that you have set. You may not use these all the time, but any time that you are setting conditions based on what the user will place into the system, you will need to work with these comparison operators.

Logical operators

You are also able to work with the operators that are known as the logical operators. These are great because they will evaluate the input that a user is giving you with the conditions that you have set. There will be three main logical operators that you may want to use, and these include the following:

- or: with this one, the compiler is going to value x, and if it is false, it will then go over and evaluate y. If x ends up being true, the compiler is going to return the evaluation of x.

- and: if x ends up being the one that is false, the compiler is going to evaluate it. If x ends up being true, it will move on and evaluate y.

- Not: if ends up being false, the compiler is going to return True. But if x ends up being true, the program will return.

These are similar to what you will find when you work with the comparison operators, but they are often used in different ways. You will only need to use the three terms above in order to make the logical operators come to life, and there are a few times when they can be extremely useful inside of your code.

assignment operators

and the last type of operator that is commonly used inside of python is known as the assignment operator. This is basically just going to use the equal sign (=) to help assign a new value over to the variable that you are working on. For example, if you are working with a variable and you want to make sure that it is equal to 100, you would just use your equal sign to make this happen. There are a lot of times when you will include this operator into the code to tell the compiler what the variable should equal, and you have probably already seen this done in some of the other codes that we have talked about. pretty much any time that you want to tell the compiler to assign a value to your variable, you will want to use the assignment operator.

There is also the possibility of being able to assign multiple values to the same variable, but you just need to make sure that you use the right signs and write it down properly in order to make this happen. You simply need to use the same variable to make this happen and then make sure that the equal sign is in the right place, and then you can have your variable hold on to as many values as you want. Most beginners choose to give one value to each variable though because this keeps things a bit simpler to handle.

as you can see, there are a lot of different operators that you are able to use, and they can really add in something extra to the code you are working with. You can add and subtract and do other things with your variable to help you do mathematical equations. You can assign a value to the variable so that the compiler has an idea of when to call it up and how to use that variable. It is even possible to make some comparisons to help you figure out how the system should work inside this program. Try out a few of the operators that we talked about in this chapter to help you add something special to your code. You may be surprised at how much you are able to do with these simple operators.

chapter 8: File Input and output

There are going to be some times when you are working on your python code and you will want to store the data that you are creating so that it is available when you want to use it later on. You will be able to store it in a few ways, whether you want to bring up just part of it or all of it later on. often, you won't need to use all of your code right in the beginning, but it is important that you have the information in order so that you can pull it up as soon as the code is ready to execute it.

as you are saving things on python, you will be able to save this file on a disk, but you can also make sure that you are reusing the code over again, as many times as you would like, inside the code you are writing. The only requirement is that you save and call up the files in the proper manner and then this can be done. This chapter is going to spend some time looking at how you would handle these files in the code so that they are saved properly, and you are able to use them when you want.

There are a few things that you can do when you decide to work with file mode inside the python code. If this is a bit confusing, there are a few ways that you can think about this. We have all done work inside of a Word document and then needed to save that document so we can find it later on. This process is similar to what you are going to do with the python language, but you will be saving parts of your code rather than the pages in a Word document. Some of the operating that you will spend your time with for these files include:

- Writing some new code to a file that you already created
- Seeking, or also moving the file over to a new location
- closing up the file
- creating a brand new file.

Each of these is going to work in order to help you have some control in what is in your files, but you need to make sure that you properly handle them. When you use these properly, you are telling your interpreter how to act. Let's take a quick look at how each of these will work when you want to save your files.

creating a New File

Before you are able to save any files, you need to take some time to create a new file that will hold onto the code that you are creating. If you want to make this new file and then be able to write on it, you need to open it up first inside of the IDE and then choose the mode that will help you to do the writing. The good news is that there will be a few options available to help you to do this. The three options that you are able to use for writing out the code include mode(x), write(w) and append(a). any time that you want to make some changes to the file that you open up, you can always use the (w) option because this is the easiest.

Now, if you would like to open up one of your files and write out a new string inside of this file, you will work with what we will call binary files. Despite this, you need to work with the write() method still. This one still works because it will make sure to return the characters that you want to write into the files and it is easier to add in the changes that you want, write out brand new content, and so much more inside the file.

For the most part, you are going to work on the write() function. This one is easy to use and will allow you to make any changes that you want inside that file. You may just want to add in some more information to this file, take stuff out, or do something else to the file once it is opened out. Now, if you would like to do the writing in the code, use this example to help you to get started:

```
#file handling operations
#writing to a new file hello.txt
f = open('hello.txt', 'w', encoding = 'utf-8')
f.write("Hello python Developers!")
f.write("Welcome to python World")
f.flush()
f.close()
```

Take the time to add this into the compiler and when it is done, you are basically making sure that all the information that you are creating will go inside the current directory. You may want to make sure that you are in a directory that will work for storage or at least one that you are able to remember. So whatever directory you are in right now is the one you will have to go back to when you are searching for the file, in this case, the hello.txt file. When you find this file in the directory and try to get it to open, you will get the message "Hello python Developers! Welcome to python World."

We went through and wrote out the program above, and so it is time to do a bit of work to make some changes in the code so you can see how that is done. You will be able to make any changes that you want to the code, but we are going to focus on changing it up to have a different thing show up on the file that we created. You are able to do this when you are writing codes inside python, you just have to change the syntax a little bit and then add in what you want to change. a good example of how you would do this is:

```
#file handling operations
#writing to a new file hello.txt
f = open('hello.txt', 'w', encoding = 'utf-8')
f.write("Hello python Developers!")
f.write("Welcome to python World")
mylist = ["apple", "orange", "Banana"]
#writelines() is used to write multiple lines into the file
f.write(mylist)
f.flush()
f.close()
```

This example is a good way to learn how to make some changes to one of the files that you already wrote out because it is simple; you just need to write out that additional line. This example is pretty basic, and you don't really need to add on that third line with the simple words, but remember that you can always use this as a syntax for your own projects and then change things around to say or do what you would like in the program.

Working With Binary Files

The next thing that we are going to concentrate on is working with binary files. When you are writing out these specific files, you want to make sure that you write out all of the data so that it is a binary file. This is pretty simple to work with inside of python because you can just take the data that you are working on and then write it out so that it becomes an image or a sound file rather than letting it be a text file. any text that you are writing inside of python can be turned into a binary file, whether you are working with a text, picture, or sound file. The thing that you have to know during this is that you need to make sure the data is located inside the object so that it can be exposed as a byte later on. If you would like to write out your text to be a binary file just use the following syntax:

```
# write binary data to a file
# writing the file hello.dat write binary mode
F = open('hello.dat', 'wb')
# writing as byte strings
f.write(b"I am writing data in binary file!/n")
f.write(b"Let's write another list/n")
f.close()
```

Before we move on, take some time to open up the compiler and write this all out. Make sure that you have the encode and decode functions in place so that it is easier to write out and even read the text out in your file for binary mode. If you want to allow this to happen inside of your code, make sure that you write out the following code example:

```
# write binary data to a file
# writing the file hello.dat write binary mode
f = open('hello.dat', 'wb')
text = "Hello World"
f.write(text.encode('utf-8'))
f.close()
```

open Up a File

Now we are going to take a look at how you can open up one of the files that you created and saved above. We already know how to make some changes to the file and even how to create that file, but this isn't going to do us much good if we are not able to go in and open up the file that we want to use. There are many times that you will want to open up your file and use it again, and a good syntax that you can use to make this happen includes:

```
# read binary data to a file
#writing the file hello.dat write append binary mode

with open("hello.dat", 'rb') as f:
        data = f.read()
        text = data.decode('utf-8'(
print(text)
```

the output that you would get from putting this into the system would be like the following:

```
Hello, world!
This is a demo using with
This file contains three lines
Hello world
This is a demo using with
```

This file contains three lines.

Seeking a File

and finally, we are going to move on to seeking one of your files. In addition to using some of the tasks above, such as creating a file, writing to the file, and opening it up, there are going to be times when you want to make a change to the file or move it around a bit. For example, if you ended up not getting things to match properly or you ended up misspelling the words in the title or placed the file in the wrong place, you will find that using the seek function can really help you out.

The seek function is going to make it easier for you to go in and change the position of your file so that it ends up in the spot that you want, or at least in a spot that is a bit easier for you to find. You will need to tell the code where it should look for the file before you can make some of these changes though, and that is where the to seek function is going to come into hand.

There are a lot of files that you can work with when you are using the python language and trying to figure out where to place a file, how to change it, and more will sometimes be difficult. Try out some of these codes and see how easy it can be to work with the files.

conclusion

Thank for making it through to the end of this book, let's hope it was informative and able to provide you with all of the tools you need to achieve your goals whatever they may be.

The next step is to start working on some of your own python codes. python is considered one of the easiest coding languages that you can learn even as a beginner because it is easy to read and the library and community can really help you along the way. This guidebook took some time to explore the various parts of the python code so that you are able to get started on writing some of your own.

There are a lot of different parts that can come with your python code and figure out how to write one of these codes can be hard without learning how to bring all the different parts together. This guidebook will discuss some of the major components that come with the python code including how to get started, how to work with the if statements, working with the exceptions, how to separate out your classes and objects, and so much more. When you are done going through some of the practice options in this guidebook, you will be an expert in working with python.

Many people are worried about getting started with the python language because they feel that it will just be too hard for them to get started. But python is so easy to learn that you will be able to get started with it right away. When you are ready to start a new coding language, make sure to read through this guidebook and learn all the basics that you need to get started.